JANE

Bodyfoods
manifesto

Healthy eating is just the beginning

CASSELL&CO

Distributed in the United States of America by Sterling Publishing Co, Inc.
387 Park Avenue South, New York, NY 10016-8810

A CIP catalogue record for this book is available from the British Library

ISBN 0-304-35465-1

Designed by Paul Saunders
Printed and bound in Great Britain by Mackays of Chatham PLC, Chatham, Kent

Cassell & Co
Wellington House
125 Strand
London WC2R 0BB

Contents

Introduction

Our lifestyles and eating habits have changed drastically over the past ten to twenty years – so drastically that they would shock our ancestors. Yet more and more people are overweight, constipated, suffering from ailments ranging from depression to cancer or living in an eating-disorder 'gaol'.

We all want good health and vitality, but how many totally healthy people do you know? Very few, I suspect. Most of us have a few little niggles, such as tiredness, headaches, sleeping or digestive problems. A body that is continually drained by working too hard, not resting and eating inappropriately is much more likely to have a suppressed immune system and therefore be susceptible to viruses and bacteria, as well as such more extreme, life-threatening conditions as heart disease and cancer.

We have to acknowledge that our bodies need respect and nourishment. Good eating habits reduce your likelihood of developing diseases and also help you to live a more enjoyable life. Take the time to think about the food that you put in your mouth and how you expect your body to cope with it and you will receive the dividends for many years to come.

The Bodyfoods ethos contained in the pages of this book will help you to choose foods that will help, rather than hinder, your body and that will inspire you to regard food as both a pleasure and one of the greatest healers on earth.

The Bodyfoods philosophy

The Bodyfoods philosophy promotes good health by helping you to understand the way in which food behaves within your body and how your life can be enhanced by the fruits that nature provides. We are forever hearing about what we shouldn't eat rather than all the things that we can enjoy. According to the Bodyfoods principle you can have virtually anything (as long as you consume it correctly) and thus eat your way to good health.

Bodyfoods are quick and easy to make

Lack of time is one of the main reasons that people give for not cooking for themselves or looking after their bodies properly. Unfortunately, many convenience foods contain substances that we would do well to avoid. Nutritious meals can be achieved as easily as popping a meal in the microwave and are both twice as delicious and much more satisfying.

Bodyfoods adapt to your lifestyle

Food has to fit into your lifestyle, and the Bodyfoods philosophy offers easy alternatives to bad eating habits, like the following.

○ A mother doesn't want to be told to count calories or to check fat contents on food labels. With the Bodyfoods approach all she needs to do is to take simple nutritional steps. For instance, instead of baking a cake with white flour and lots of sugar she could use wholewheat flour and natural sweeteners, such as sultanas or dates soaked in fresh orange juice.

○ By following the Bodyfoods philosophy only 80 per cent of the time – for example, by choosing a fresh vegetable soup or a spinach and orange salad for lunch and by cutting down on coffee – busy business people will not only look good, but also feel good.

Bodyfoods are good value

Healthy eating does not make your shopping bills higher. Not only are simple foods usually less expensive than fast foods weight for weight, but by promoting good health they also reduce the cost of sick leave and the number of productive working hours lost by feeling sleepy and exhausted during the day.

Bodyfoods are sensual foods

As we struggle with the stresses of modern living we often forget the sheer sensory enjoyment of eating. Our mouths, eyes, ears and noses should be titillated if we are to savour our food and thereby remain healthy. We glean the most satisfaction from foods with a high organoleptic quality: in other words, they stimulate more than one sense (think of sizzling bacon or the bubbling of a thick soup). So banish tasteless, boring foods from your life and replace them with tasty, irresistible dishes that you really want to eat.

Bodyfoods are addictive

By respecting your body and feeding it with good food you will enable it to perform well. This book tells you how to break your old, unbalanced eating habits and instead form new, healthy ones. Many people think that they are familiar with all that there is to know about healthy eating, low-fat and high-fibre diets, but they are often so fed up with hearing about what they can't eat that food becomes the enemy. By instead focusing on all the marvellous foods that they can enjoy and understanding how they can re-educate their bodies to use foods efficiently they will gain confidence that they will achieve their health goals.

Bodyfoods can make your body self-sufficient

By following the Bodyfoods ethos you can stimulate your body to become self-sufficient, reducing the need for artificial supplements and unnatural, symptom-masking drugs.

Rebuild your life with Bodyfoods

Eating well enables the body to build up a reserve of nutrients for those occasions when there simply isn't the time to eat properly. If 80 per cent of your meals are nutritious your body will be able to withstand the odd period of nutrient strain. In addition, the Bodyfoods way helps you to prepare your body for the future.

Learn to love food!

Remember that although it is healthy to make positive choices about the food and drink that you consume your life should not revolve around food alone. Overly focusing on food and controlling your eating habits can become an obsession, which can far too easily escalate into an eating disorder, such as anorexia or bulimia, if you have underlying insecurities, too.

1. The Bodyfoods Lifestyle

If anything is sacred, the human body is sacred.
WALT WHITMAN (1855–81), 'I Sing the Body Electric'

Respect your body

Food, in conjunction with the digestive system, provides the body with all of the nutrients that it needs: the 'fuel' that we need for life and health. Try to think of the stomach as the centre of the body and not just as something that takes whatever we throw at it. The body is like a finely tuned engine that can work amazingly well if maintained and fuelled appropriately. It must therefore be respected and not abused.

If we ate only easily available, fast food, we would end up consuming vast amounts of fat, sugar and grossly overprocessed ingredients. In time we would not only feel lousy but would also develop disease. If you get the combination of foods that you consume right you can feel marvellous, but if you get them wrong your body will complain.

Keeping a food diary can tell us a great deal about what you are eating and whether or not it is fuelling your body effectively. Being aware of the foods that you are eating and how your nutritional status can be improved can cure many common ailments before any medical treatment is undertaken. Indeed, many people are able to cope without medication, or at least reduce their dependency on it, once they have learned to eat nutritious foods.

Your body's response to food

By understanding how your appetite mechanism works and the concepts of hunger and satiety (the feeling that you get when you're contentedly full) you will be able to feel well after eating, both in body and mind.

Signalling to the brain

There are four main stages during eating when you send signals to the 'satiety' centre of the brain: when your taste buds are stimulated; when lifting your arm to eat; when chewing; and when your stomach receives food.

o Both taste and tactile stimulation within the mouth lead to greater satiety. If a meal contains exciting flavours, along with varying temperatures and textures, your mouth has a greater opportunity to register satisfaction. The foods that have the highest satisfaction value are those with several organoleptic properties – in other words, they stimulate more than one sense: they look good, smell good, feel good in the mouth, taste good and even sound good. If you eat similar foods all the time your mouth gets used to their tastes and textures, while if you introduce variety into your diet, and also choose food that you love, the production of saliva and other digestive juices increases.

o The more often you lift your hand to your mouth in order to deliver food to it the greater your eventual satiety.

o There are stretch receptors within the jaw which respond when you chew. The more you chew and the more time you take over eating the greater your brain's perception of satiety. So take smaller mouthfuls and have little breaks while you're eating a meal. Eat slowly and cut the food into small pieces with a knife and fork.

○ When there is food in your stomach stretch receptors within the stomach wall send signals of fullness to your brain. If you eat foods that are low in bulk (like fatty, sugary or refined foods and alcohol), they pass through your stomach quickly, which means that few signals are sent to the satiety centre in the brain and you are therefore likely to eat more before you feel satisfied. The opposite happens when you eat high-fibre foods, such as fresh fruit and vegetables, pulses and wholegrain bread, pasta and rice. Because high-fibre foods have thick cell walls and are therefore more difficult for the body to break down they stay in the stomach for a lot longer, swell and send numerous signals to the brain's satiety centre, making you feel full and contented.

When should you eat?

Not everyone feels hungry at the same time and you may also find that your hormone and stress levels affect whether or not you feel hungry. There's no hard-and-fast rule about when you should eat – it's just a question of working out how your body responds to food and how you can eat to maximise your performance and overall health. Take a little time to think about what your daily schedule demands and how you can choose foods to meet your body's needs. The best way in which to do this is to keep a 'food-and-mood' diary. Write down what you eat and how you feel in the morning, after lunch and in the evening.

Before changing your eating habits you need to consider all of the evidence.

Although it is good to get into the habit of having three meals a day, these don't have to be three large meals at set times. See how your body responds to eating three or five meals a day and then try to build a healthy, regular eating pattern around your conclusions. Yet however many meals you have during the day you shouldn't go for long periods without eating. Not only can this harm the digestive system by exposing it to acids produced by the stomach, but it can also make you feel desperately hungry and therefore more inclined either to eat inappropriately or to overeat. Regular snacks are preferable to starving yourself and then eating a large meal.

Remember, too, that the digestive system needs a plentiful supply of oxygen to enable it to work properly. If you rush around immediately after eating, or eat on the move, oxygen is diverted from the stomach to other muscles, which hinders digestion. Our bodies try to stop us from doing this by releasing hormones that make us feel sleepy immediately after a meal. Don't fight this – you don't have to sleep, just rest for ten to fifteen minutes.

Enjoy your food

Food's place in your life should always be kept in perspective. Food should not become an obsession or something that is used as the only tool of affection. Yet because it is one of the few things that we can control in life food can become a destructive weapon to be wielded against us, sowing the seeds of a future eating disorder.

Above all, don't let food become a negative issue: think of all the wonderful things that you can eat that provide pleasure and comfort. Indeed, when you think about, choose and eat the food and drink that you like the production of saliva increases.

Instead of regarding eating as just a quick nutrient fix, think of it as an enjoyable pastime. It is not only how food tastes, but also how it stimulates our eyes that help us to decide whether we want to eat it or not. So value meals not only for their content, but also for their setting. Lay the table with candles for a relaxing touch or have breakfast in bed. Taking time to think about the presentation of food can start the saliva flowing. Envisage contrasting colours, shapes and textures. The size of the plate is important, too: food should neither appear lost or crowded on it. If you are overweight you may often find it difficult to leave food on your plate; serving smaller portions can make you stop and question whether you need a second helping.

Guilt-free eating

Eating without guilt is my most important doctrine. All foods, including chocolate, can be incorporated into a healthy-eating lifestyle (unless there is a proven negative reaction to them, such as an allergy, and even then you should be able to find equally tempting alternatives). Denying yourself or your family members of it will only increase the likelihood of bingeing on the forbidden food. Establishing a balance by basing 90 per cent of your meals around healthy foods allows you occasionally to indulge in foods that you know are a little over the top. Eat and enjoy, but remember to get back on a healthier nutritional track the next day.

Special diets

It is particularly vital that anyone on a special diet should not feel deprived of 'normal' food. They should instead enjoy the same food as their friends or family as far as possible. For example, rather than telling hyperactive children that they can't have commercially produced ice lollies their parents could make lollies for all of their children with freshly squeezed orange and grapefruit juice. Similarly, baking a date and walnut cake made with wholemeal flour instead of a sugar-loaded Madeira cake will make a diabetic feel much less isolated. If you have a wheat intolerance, there are also lots of dishes that all of the family can enjoy, such as risottos and buckwheat pancakes, as well as sauces thickened with potato flour instead of wheat flour.

2. Eating well

*One cannot think well,
love well, sleep well, if one has not dined well.*
VIRGINIA WOOLF (1882–1942), A Room of One's Own

What your body needs

In the grand plan of looking, feeling and staying well one of the first things to consider is how you can give your body the nutrients that it needs. A healthy-eating lifestyle provides all of the necessary nutrients to enable the body to execute daily tasks with ease. It is therefore important to know which types of food you should eat, and why, when structuring a healthy-eating plan.

We all need a combination of foods from the main nutritional groups: carbohydrates, proteins and fats. Within these foods are found vitamins, minerals and other compounds that are important to our health and well-being. Once you have identified the sources of nutrients that you really enjoy eating you can think about incorporating these foods into your day-to-day life.

Carbohydrates

Along with fats, carbohydrates provide our bodies with energy; not just the 'visible' energy that we use in moving about, but also the energy that fuels the many processes that are constantly going on within our bodies.

There are two types of carbohydrate: sugar and starch, both of which can be refined or found in a more natural form.

o Natural sugars are found in fruit and vegetables.

o Refined sugars (including honey and both white and brown sugar) are found in soft drinks, cakes, biscuits, jams, jellies and sweets.

o Natural starches are found in wholegrain and wholemeal breakfast cereals, wholemeal flour and bread, wholewheat pasta, brown rice, potatoes and yams, lentils, chickpeas and beans, bananas and plantains, nuts, sweetcorn, parsnips and other root vegetables.

o Refined starches are found in sugary, processed breakfast cereals, white flour and white bread, white pasta, white rice, biscuits and cakes.

Although refined carbohydrates are not in themselves bad for us, they don't enable the body to work as efficiently as the unrefined or natural types.

When making up your daily eating plan you should base each of your meals on a starchy food, such as potato, rice, beans, pasta or bread, which provides energy at a slower, steadier rate than sugary foods.

If you are worried about putting on weight, remember that starchy foods are not fattening in themselves; problems arise when you load them with butter or deep-fry them or, like most foods, when you eat them to excess.

Proteins

Protein is needed to help the body to build strong muscles, repair tissues and maintain effective immune and hormonal systems.

Proteins are absorbed into the blood as amino acids, of which there are two types: essential and non-essential. The body can produce non-essential amino acids from other sources, but essential amino acids are obtained directly from food.

o Meat, poultry, game, fish and shellfish, eggs and dairy products, as well as soya products (like soya milk and tofu), contain all of the essential amino acids.

o Beans and other pulses, grains, nuts, seeds and manufactured vegetable-protein foods contain protein, but don't include all of the essential amino acids. However, in combination they can be used by the body to meet its daily protein requirements.

Too little protein can compromise health by stunting growth in children or causing a loss in muscle mass in older people. A more common problem for many adults is too much protein, however, which is stored as fat if too much is consumed.

It's best to choose a lean protein rather than fatty meats. The average adult should eat a piece of lean protein about the size of a breast of chicken for their main meal, plus an additional portion half this size in a smaller meal or snack. A good intake of milk and other dairy products provides protein, calcium and the vitamins B2 and B12, among other nutrients. Adults should therefore try to consume 600ml (1 pint) of milk or its equivalent each day.

Fats

Although excess fat has been linked to many health problems, some fat is essential in everyone's diet. Foods that contain fats provide not only a concentrated source of energy, but also the fat-soluble vitamins A, D, E and K, which are vital for the development and maintenance of a healthy body and mind.

Fats help the body to fulfil specific functions, like energy production, hormone metabolism or tissue repair. The body also needs to store some fat in order to prevent excessive loss of body heat (this is especially important for babies). Fat is additionally required to produce and carry the sex hormones testosterone, oestrogen and progesterone around the body. Too little body fat can interfere with your libido and cause women to stop menstruating; it can also make you more prone to developing osteoporosis. Excess fat, on the other hand, usually leads to an increase in the amount of fat that is deposited in the blood-vessel linings, which can cause serious problems like heart disease.

There are two main types of fat: saturated and unsaturated. Unsaturated fats can be further divided into mono- and polyunsaturated fats. The fact that they are metabolised in slightly different ways means that we can bring about positive health changes by choosing one type of fat in preference to another.

o Saturated fats are generally considered to be the 'bad' fats. They are solid at room temperature and come mainly from such animal products as butter, lard, suet and dripping, meat, eggs, full-fat milk, cheese and full-fat yoghurt. They are also found in hard margarines, which contain trans-fatty acids. Most cakes, biscuits, and pastry, which are generally made with butter or hard margarine, are therefore likely to be high in saturated fats, as are coconut oil and palm oil.

o Unsaturated fats are better for your body. They are generally liquid at room temperature and come from vegetable sources, like such oils as olive, sunflower, safflower, rapeseed, soya, grapeseed, peanut and sesame. They are also found in soft margarines labelled 'high in polyunsaturates' and in oily fish like herring, sardines, mackerel and trout.

Children need some fat in their diets – it is just a question of quantity and balance. For adults, the balance is provided by making sure that you include plenty of fibre in your diet. We should all watch our total fat intake, whether it be from animal or vegetable sources, and keep the quantity low.

Unless you have a medically diagnosed cholesterol problem, choose the fat that you like, whether it's butter or olive oil, but use it in small amounts. I don't generally recommend margarine and low-fat spreads because they often contain hydrogenated vegetable oil, which can cause free-radical damage within the body's cells.

Fibre

Fibre is one of the most exciting areas of nutritional research and the messages that have been drawn from this research are nearly all positive.

o Fibre stimulates the bowel to excrete waste products on a regular basis.

o It ensures that the absorption of nutrients from foods occurs in a controlled and gradual fashion, thereby avoiding energy and mood crashes.

o It stimulates the body to produce substances that limit free-radical damage.

In addition to these benefits, soluble fibre (which is found in fruit and vegetables, oats and pulses) can reduce the amount of cholesterol that you absorb from food. Eating a high-fibre diet can decrease your risk of developing digestive disorders, constipation, certain types of cancer and heart disease, too.

The main providers of fibre in our diet are cereals (edible grains), such as wheat, corn (maize), oats and rice and foods made from them, preferably wholegrain or wholemeal types, including bread, pasta and breakfast cereals. The other great fibre-providers are vegetables (including fresh or dried beans and lentils, known as pulses) and fruit.

If the fibre is going to work efficiently within your body you need to drink at least 2 litres (4 pints) of water every day (that is the adult requirement; you should generally respond to your children's thirst and encourage them to drink a lot of fluid). Water helps the fibre to swell and carry out its functions.

The only drawback is that an excess of fibre can hinder the release of energy, so you should include some lower-fibre starches (like bread, pasta, rice and other cereals), cheeses, nuts (and peanut butter), olive oil, bananas and avocados in your diet.

Vitamins and minerals
Most healthy people do not need vitamin and mineral supplements as long as they are eating a wide range of fresh foods, are

drinking sufficient water and are not consuming excessive amounts of tea, coffee or cola-based drinks.

There are two types of vitamins: water-soluble vitamins (C and B complex) and fat-soluble vitamins (A, D, E and K). Water-soluble vitamins cannot be stored by the body, so foods containing these should be eaten daily. They can also be destroyed by overcooking, especially by boiling vegetables or fruit in lots of water.

Note that the daily adult requirement figures given below are specified by the Department of Health and apply only to the UK.

Vitamin A

Vital for: growth, healthy skin and hair, good vision and healthy tooth enamel.

Found in: animal products, such as liver and liver products like pâté and kidneys; oily fish, such as herring, mackerel and trout; fish-liver oils; milk; cheese (apart from low-fat cheese); butter and margarine; egg yolks.

Daily adult requirement: 600–700 micrograms.

Important note: never take a vitamin A preparation or supplement without medical supervision as it can build up in the liver and cause serious damage.

Vitamin B complex

Includes: B1 (thiamin), B2 (riboflavin), B3 (nicotinic acid), B5 (pantothenic acid), B6 (pyridoxine), B12 (cobalamin) and folate (folic acid).

Vital for: the development and maintenance of a healthy nervous system; the digestion of food and its conversion into energy; the production of red blood cells; some maintain a healthy brain, immune system, skin, hair, teeth, gums, blood vessels and the lining of the nose and throat.

Found in: animal products, such as liver, kidneys and meat, especially meat juices; yeast; milk; yoghurt; cheese; eggs; fish; brown rice, other wholegrain cereals and wheatgerm; green vegetables, such as asparagus, broccoli and spinach; potatoes; nuts; pulses; bananas; dried fruits, like apricots, dates and figs.

Daily adult requirement: B1: 0.7–1.1 milligrams; B2: 1.3–1.8 milligrams; B3: 15–21 milligrams; B5: 3–7 milligrams; B6: 1.2–1.4 milligrams; B12: 1.5 micrograms; folate: 200–500 micrograms.

Important note: a general vitamin B complex supplement helps the vitamins to be better absorbed.

Vitamin C

Vital for: growth; healthy body tissue; the healing of wounds; the absorption of iron; preventing or reducing the severity of the common cold.

Found in: vegetables, such as broccoli, spinach, curly kale, Brussels sprouts, spring greens, cabbage, cauliflower, red, green and yellow peppers, watercress, potatoes, green peas and mangetout; fruits like oranges, strawberries, kiwis, grapefruit and other citrus fruits, blackcurrants, rosehips, guavas, mangoes, papayas, lychees, raspberries, nectarines and peaches.

Daily adult requirement: 60 milligrams.

Important note: vitamin C is a water-soluble vitamin which the body cannot store in excessive amounts; taking it to excess can cause sensitive and irritable stomachs and mouth ulcers.

Vitamin D
Vital for: healthy bones and teeth, in conjunction with calcium.
Found in: oily fish, such as tuna, mackerel and sardines; cod-liver oil; liver; eggs; butter and margarine; cheese; milk; yoghurt.
Daily adult requirement: no supplement required, except for some older people.

Vitamin E
Vital for: developing and maintaining strong cells, especially in the blood; reducing the risk of heart disease and some cancers.
Found in: fruits, such as avocados, blackberries and mangoes; vegetables like tomatoes, sweet potatoes, spinach and watercress; nuts and seeds; wheatgerm and wholegrain cereals; soft margarine and vegetable oils like sunflower, safflower, corn and olive oil.
Daily adult requirement: 3–4 milligrams.

Vitamin K
Vital for: helping the blood to clot to the naturally healthy degree; maintaining strong bones.
Found in: most vegetables; wholegrain cereals; live yoghurt (but we mainly produce it in our guts, with the aid of healthy bacteria).
Daily adult requirement: no supplement required.

Calcium
Vital for: forming strong, healthy bones and teeth; the prevention of osteoporosis.
Found in: dairy produce, such as cows', goats' and sheep's milk,

cheese, cream and yoghurt; green, leafy vegetables like spinach, curly kale, watercress and broccoli; okra; tofu; pulses; dried figs and apricots; oysters; canned fish with soft, edible bones (sardines, salmon, pilchards and mackerel); sesame seeds and tahini; almonds, Brazil nuts and hazelnuts; some breads and flour.

Daily adult requirement: 800 milligrams.

Iron

Vital for: healthy blood and muscles; preventing anaemia.

Found in: lean, red meat; game; liver and kidneys; eggs; spinach, curly kale, watercress, broccoli, Savoy cabbage and other dark-green, leafy vegetables; lentils, beans and peas; oily fish, such as tuna, mackerel and sardines; oysters; dried fruits, especially figs, raisins, apricots and prunes; canned blackcurrants; wholegrain cereals and wholemeal bread; black treacle; nuts; liquorice; plain chocolate.

Daily adult requirement: 8–15 milligrams.

Magnesium

Vital for: building strong bones, teeth and muscles; regulating body temperature; releasing energy; helping the body to absorb and metabolise other vitamins and minerals.

Found in: wholegrain cereal products, such as wholemeal and granary bread, wholewheat pasta and brown rice; nuts and seeds; pulses; green, leafy vegetables, as well as okra, peas, sweetcorn, courgettes and parsnips; milk and yoghurt; lean meat; dried figs, apricots and raisins; bananas.

Daily adult requirement: no supplement required.

Potassium

Vital for: regulating the body's water balance, heart rhythm, nerve impulses and muscle function, along with sodium.

Found in: potatoes; bananas and other fresh fruits; orange juice; dried apricots and prunes.

Daily adult requirement: 3.5 grams.

Zinc

Vital for: maintaining a healthy immune system.

Found in: shellfish, such as oysters, crab, mussels and lobster; canned sardines; turkey, duck and goose; lean meats like beef, lamb, gammon, pork and venison; liver and kidneys; Parmesan and other hard or crumbly cheeses; eggs; wholegrain breads and brown rice; nuts and seeds; wheatgerm and wholegrain cereals; pulses; fresh peas; watercress, spinach and asparagus; dried apricots, figs and raisins; passion fruit.

Daily adult requirement: 15 milligrams.

Selenium

Vital for: maintaining a healthy liver.

Found in: Brazil and cashew nuts; sunflower seeds; wholewheat bread; milk; hard, crumbly cheeses; eggs; chicken; lean meat and offal; fish and shellfish.

Daily adult requirement: no supplement required.

Antioxidants

Antioxidants are a group of substances that includes vitamins C and E, along with beta-carotene (which the body converts into vitamin A) and the minerals selenium and zinc. They are believed to reduce the likelihood of developing cancer and heart disease, as well as other diseases of ageing, like arthritis and cataracts. They do this in several ways:

o by boosting the immune system;

o by producing anti-cancer substances;

o by preventing blood fats from oxidising and leaving deposits in the blood vessels;

o through their antioxidant activity.

Although our bodies need oxygen, the process of oxidation can be harmful because it results in the unstable molecules known as free radicals, which interact with those that make up the body's cells, causing damage that can lead to disease.

In order to take in all of the antioxidants that you need, you should eat an all-round, antioxidant-rich diet that includes plenty of the foods listed above, below the relevant headings. Fruit and vegetables also contain another type of antioxidant called bioflavonoids, which are concentrated in the peel, skin or outer layers of plants.

Bacteria

Bacteria are not all bad, and the healthy gut contains colonies of bacteria that serve a number of functions. They are the principal producers of vitamin K, for example, and also generate a certain amount of energy. They furthermore produce substances that may be beneficial in preventing many diseases and in generally improving the immune system. You should therefore include some bacteria in your daily diet (particularly if you have been taking antibiotics, which kill the 'good' bacteria in the gut and expose it to an overgrowth of 'bad' bacteria).

The two most beneficial gut bacteria are acidophilus and bifidus. Taking regular quantities of these helps to replenish stocks of gut bacteria and frequently causes adverse bowel symptoms to disappear. Both acidophilus and bifidus are most easily and effectively absorbed from natural yoghurt, particularly 'live' or 'bio' yoghurts. A good daily dosage would be 20 milligrams, which can usually be found in a small pot of yoghurt. People who have a sensitive immune system or gut, however, should seek advice from their doctor before taking these bacteria, as they are potential gut-irritants.

A healthy-eating lifestyle

Once you recognise that your body needs a well-balanced diet, you need to know how to put a healthy-eating lifestyle into practice. Build your knowledge – and health – on the following guidelines.

Water is best!

Although humans can survive for quite some time without food, we can live for only a few days without water. Water is needed to flush waste products out of the body; to keep the skin, hair and organs healthy; to produce digestive enzymes; and to enable the body to glean all of the essential nutrients from the food and drink that we consume by helping them to flow from the food into the body. In a healthy diet water is closely associated with fibre: it assists the fibre to swell, stimulates the walls of the gut and helps to prevent constipation.

Most adults should try to drink 2 to 3 litres (about 4 or 5 pints) of water every day. Urine is one of the best guides to the adequacy of your fluid intake: your urine should be pale in colour, and you should go to the loo regularly throughout the day. Any fresh-fruit juice or shake that you drink on top of this recommended daily requirement will round up your fluid requirement. (A glass of fruit juice a day is enough for adults, as it contains large amounts of natural sugar, and therefore calories.) When you want a hot drink, consider a herbal or fruit tea.

Although carbonated drinks are not bad in themselves, they have a number of drawbacks that you should look out for.

o Many cola-based drinks contain caffeine, whose intake should be restricted. Your consumption of tea and coffee should also be limited to three cups a day.

o The majority of such drinks are high in sugar. Although the label may call the sugar dextrose, fructose, glucose or sucrose, these can all cause energy-balance problems, headaches, mood swings, weight problems, tooth decay and ratty moods in children.

o 'Diet' drinks contain artificial sweeteners and additives that are not especially harmful in small amounts yet are not as good or refreshing as pure water.

Strategies for healthy eating

Here are some further helpful tips and pointers.

○ In order to gain the maximum benefit from the fibre, vitamins and minerals that they contain, you should eat five good-sized portions of fresh fruit or vegetables every day. A combination of raw and cooked is best.

○ Too much refined sugar disrupts your natural energy balance and can cause headaches, mood swings and, if eaten in large quantities, hyperglycaemia. It is much better to get into the habit of using the natural sugars in fruits to provide sweetness. Make fruit shakes or purée fruits to spread on bread or use as a sauce.

○ I believe that organic produce is generally preferable to the alternative because no pesticides and chemicals have been used in its production. The fewer chemicals that we put into our bodies the healthier we will be. However, you should consider a products overall healthiness (the fat and sugar content), before deciding that it is healthy. Organic doesn't always mean healthy – it usually means healthier.

○ You should ideally eat three meals a day: breakfast, a smaller snack or lunch-type meal and one main meal. Meals should be based on carbohydrates, fruit and/or vegetables. The main meal should include a source of lean protein, along with carbohydrates and plenty of vegetables and fruit. Choose lean sources of protein, which meet your body's protein requirements without overloading it with fat.

○ The practice of eating proteins and carbohydrates at the same meal is known as 'food combining', while eating proteins and carbohydrates separately is called 'food separating'. There is no physiological reasoning behind food combining, and I believe that you should not have to agonise over whether you are 'allowed' to eat certain things at certain times.

o Before you put anything into your mouth ask yourself three questions: 'Do I want it? Do I like it? Do I need it?' If you want it and like it, then go ahead and enjoy it; if you don't, why bother wasting the eating experience?

Feeding children

A well-balanced diet, a healthy lifestyle and a positive relationship with food are among the best gifts that you can give your child.

Your child will imitate your eating habits, along with your likes and dislikes. It is therefore important to establish good and consistent eating habits – for all the family – when your child is young. Here are a few tips which may help you to do so.

o Try to give your child a varied diet. If you serve the same things every day, boredom will soon set in.

o Take your child shopping. Knowing where produce come from is an important tool in food appreciation, and enthusiasm on your part will rub off on your child. Even if you can only get to supermarkets, talk about different foods and their seasonality.

o Use convenience foods wisely. Don't dismiss all tinned, frozen and packet foods as being nutritionally inferior to fresh. It's much more important for you to be relaxed at the table than to turn meal times into a military-style exercise.

○ Make food fun! Encourage your child to spend time with you while you're cooking.

○ Sit down to eat with your child whenever possible. Even if you are going to eat your main meal later, have a drink or snack with your child.

○ Ensure that there are no distractions – like the television – at meal times. This will allow your child to concentrate on foods and flavours, as well as to relax and communicate.

○ Encourage your child to eat slowly. Rushed children frequently become obese adults who don't notice what they eat. Bolting their meals can also cause them to develop stress-induced indigestion in later life.

○ Try not to give the impression that dessert is the best part of the meal.

○ The best way in which to deal with any food fad is to ignore it. If you make a fuss, your child will associate food with conflict and may develop a lifelong dislike of certain foods.

If your child is not eating much at the meal table, check that they are not filling themselves up with drinks and/or snacks between meals. You may be able to encourage your child to eat by:

○ introducing unfamiliar foods without comment;

○ serving a food that they say they don't like in a different way, again without comment;

○ using different textures in foods (like making lean minced meat into sausages);

o devising novel ways of eating (theme meals and picnics, for example);

o involving your child in the preparation of meals.

If your child is overweight, don't put them on a restricted diet – they must eat a variety of healthy foods in order to ingest all of the nutrients that they need. Remember that a high-fibre diet gives a great deal of satiety, and provide your child with plenty of vegetables and fruits, a variety of breads (mainly wholemeal) and the occasional, fruit-based dessert.

Strengthening bones and teeth

As a person grows from infancy into adulthood, their bones evolve, becoming harder until their late teens. Then the process is reversed: after the age of twenty the bones begin to lose their density. Although childhood is therefore the most important time for bone growth, once you are past your teens you should still ensure that your body receives adequate levels of certain essential nutrients for bone maintenance, chiefly calcium, which needs the support of vitamins D and K, magnesium and several other minerals.

The foods that help you to build and maintain strong teeth are also those that are rich in calcium, vitamin D and magnesium. The most important nutrients for gums are vitamins A, B complex and C, as well as zinc.

Sugar is the biggest single cause of tooth decay, and artificial sweeteners can be just as damaging. You should always rinse your mouth with water after a fruit snack or drink because it may contain acid that attacks tooth enamel. Both adults' and children's dental health can also benefit from the following tips.

o Keep your teeth and gums healthy by chewing on foods like toast, pitta bread, raw vegetables and fruit.

o Avoid sweets that remain in the mouth for a long time; eat sweets soon after meals and then brush your teeth.

o Don't eat or drink anything other than water after you have cleaned your teeth at night.

Nourishing skin, hair and nails

Adverse changes in either the balance of nutrients that you are ingesting or your general health quickly show in your skin, as skin cells have a very short life span, being replaced every few days. If you want your skin to look good, it needs a regular supply of water, nutrients and oxygen. A well-balanced diet provides it with nutrients and oxygen, and you should also drink plenty of water, because one of the most common causes of tired, unhealthy-looking skin is dehydration.

Fresh fruits and vegetables contain a huge array of skin-replenishing vitamins and minerals, as well as providing additional water. Boost your intake of the fruits and vegetables that contain the vitamin A precursor beta-carotene.

The skin is the nurturing bed for both hair and nails, so it is vital to look after it well. Your hair reflects your general state of health, and it is therefore important to look to your lifestyle if you want to keep it in good condition. One of the simplest ways in which to improve the look of your hair is to drink more water and to avoid caffeine.

It is rare that a deficiency in any one nutrient can cause poor nails, but in some cases they can signify health problems, such as iron-deficiency anaemia or liver problems. Severe calcium deficiency can manifest itself in brittle nails, which often respond well to an increased intake of biotin.

Boosting energy

There are varying degrees of lack of energy, from normal weariness to debilitating, chronic fatigue. By keeping a food, drink and symptom diary for a week or two you will be able to see whether there are any patterns to your lack of energy and therefore whether you can adjust your eating plan to address them.

The main nutritional causes of loss of energy include:

o a lack of the correct nutrients;

o anaemia;

o food intolerances;

o too much caffeine, alcohol or nicotine;

o lack of oxygen in the blood;

o a mismatch between food intake and natural biorhythms and lifestyle demands.

Include fresh vegetables and fruit, lean proteins, wholegrain foods, dairy products and plenty of water in your daily eating plan. Try to cut out processed, ready-made and high-fat fast foods and reduce your caffeine, alcohol and nicotine consumption drastically.

If you feel that your diet is already well balanced but your energy levels are not as high as they should be, ask your doctor to arrange a series of blood tests to find out whether you have any nutritional deficiencies. In the case of a mild deficiency, you can increase your intake of the food sources of the relevant nutrient. If you have a serious deficiency, you should consult a dietitian for advice about supplements.

Building up the immune system

A strong immune system will help your body to ward off infections, but your natural immunity may be lowered as a result of a virus, another illness or stress, or simply when you are chronically tired. It's therefore well worth building up your immune system.

Here are some helpful guidelines to follow.

o Eat a well-balanced diet, including fresh fruit, vegetables and pulses, wholegrains, lean protein, dairy products and water.

o Ensure that you are ingesting the recommended amounts of vitamin C, zinc and magnesium, all of which help to maintain a healthy immune system.

o Avoid eating foods that are well past their 'use by' dates, and store and cook foods according to food-safety regulations.

o Get enough sleep. Sleep requirements vary, and it's not just the quantity of sleep that counts. If you go to bed early, you are more likely to enjoy the most therapeutic type of sleep.

o Try to reduce the level of stress in your life. The benefits of boosting your nutritional status are reduced if you are stressed.

o Stop smoking, as this damages your lungs and reduces your ability to fight infections.

o If you have been prescribed antibiotics, make sure that you are eating well and try to have a small pot of 'live' yoghurt, containing bifidus and acidophilus, every day, which will help to keep your gut flora healthy.

Menstruation

Many women suffer from unpleasant symptoms during their menstrual cycle. Although no particular food can cure period problems, what, and how, you eat can have a profound effect on the severity of such symptoms.

Women who eat a well-balanced diet generally seem to suffer less from pre-menstrual tension (PMT) than those who eat lots of sugary and convenience foods and drink too much tea or coffee. Include foods that are rich in all of the B vitamins (including dairy produce, eggs, wholegrain foods and green, leafy vegetables like watercress and spinach) in your diet.

If you suffer from weight gain before a period, you need to ascertain whether the swelling is due to excess fluid, fat or gas (or all three) before changing your diet. The most common cause of weight gain is a temporary increase in fluid retention, and the following strategies may help to control it:

o keep your salt intake low;

o drink plenty of water;

o eat potassium-rich foods;

o avoid caffeine and other diuretics.

If your abdomen is bloated, it may be filled with gas, which may be caused by either bread or dairy produce or sugary or salty foods. Eating a pot of 'live' yoghurt a day may help to redress the bacterial balance in your gut.

If you suffer from breast and period pain, try taking the following measures:

o keep your diet low in saturated fats;

o increase your intake of oily fish;

o consider taking evening-primrose oil.

Conception

There are three key issues to address when planning a pregnancy: body weight, alcohol consumption and vitamin and mineral intake.

Women's weight takes on an increased significance when they are planning to become pregnant. When their amount of body fat is low they may have problems in both conceiving and carrying a healthy baby to term. Overweight women may also find it difficult to conceive because their excess body fat may interfere with ovulation.

Excessive alcohol intake in both men and women can lead to decreased sexual sensitivity, reduced fertility in women and impotence in men. Women should keep their alcohol consumption down to no more than one unit a day, though men may drink a maximum of twenty-eight units a week.

Protein and fat consumption are as important as vitamin and mineral ingestion, as low intakes of either protein or fat may lead to impaired fertility. Certain nutrients – folic acid, iron, zinc and manganese – are especially important in aiding conception.

o Mothers who are deficient in folic acid are at increased risk of having a baby with such neural-tube defects as spina bifida. Ensure that your diet is rich in folic acid and also take a supplement of 400 micrograms for three months before and after conception.

o Deficiencies in iron, zinc and manganese can lead to low libido and sterility in both partners or birth defects in the baby, so eat plenty of foods that contain these nutrients.

Pregnancy

The first thing to do when you become pregnant is to evaluate your diet and see whether any improvements are needed. Many women make the mistake of overnourishing themselves. Although your body does have an increased demand for vitamins and minerals, it becomes more efficient during pregnancy, absorbing more of the nutrients and using more of the calories that you take in. Other than folic acid, vitamin and mineral supplements could be harmful to your developing baby, and its nutritional needs can easily be met as long as you follow a healthy, well-balanced diet that is:

o rich in high-fibre carbohydrates;

o low in fats and refined sugars;

o moderate in lean proteins;

o rich in fresh fruits and vegetables;

o low in alcohol.

Although you don't need to 'eat for two', you must eat enough to ensure that your baby grows, and also that you remain strong during the pregnancy and after the birth. Obey your appetite and eat what you fancy, but make sure that you take in enough iron, vitamin C and calcium.

If you suffer from morning sickness, try the following strategies:

o check the strength of your iron supplement;

o don't go for long periods without eating;

o don't drink too much tea or coffee; instead try rice water, peppermint, ginger or camomile tea and some fizzy drinks (sipped slowly);

o avoid fatty foods;

o experiment with the temperature of your foods;

o nibble a biscuit (try a ginger one) before getting up.

Nutrition in middle age

Middle age is the time to make an added investment in your health, taking time to boost your nutritional status and to ensure that you are doing everything possible to stay fit. Both men and women should particularly address the nutritional and lifestyle issues surrounding heart disease: what you eat and drink, your body weight and blood-fat level, exercise and smoking.

For many people middle age is a transitional period. The body is furthermore experiencing changes in metabolism that may alter the usual pattern of weight gain and bring about digestive problems and sleeping difficulties. The ageing process most noticeably affects the appearance of the hair and skin, however.

Many people find that their gut's behaviour changes quite significantly as they enter middle age. They begin to suffer from bloating, constipation, indigestion and diarrhoea. This occurs because the muscles and glands in the digestive system are very sensitive to blood-hormone levels, and at certain times of life, like in middle age, your gut varies in its ability to absorb and metabolise the nutrients in the food that you eat.

'Middle-age spread', or weight gain, may also occur. Although there is admittedly a change in the body's metabolism, an increase in body weight, especially fat, can only come from an excess of unused calories. By adopting a healthy-eating plan your weight problem should be minimised. Do not, however, lose too much weight, because rapid weight loss can predispose you to an increased risk of stroke, heart problems and depression (and, in women, osteoporosis). Above all, it is essential not to allow your body to become malnourished by going on crash diets.

Some middle-aged women can suffer from quite severe fluid retention, especially if they are on hormone-replacement therapy (HRT). Men who suffer from fluid retention usually do so as a result of circulatory problems. If you are worried about this, see your doctor and don't take any diuretics (unless they have been prescribed by him or her), because these can seriously disturb your fluid, vitamin and mineral balances. If your doctor prescribes diuretics, make sure that your diet is well balanced and contains lots of fresh fruit, vegetables and wholegrain products. Nutritionally, you can tackle fluid retention in the following ways.

○ Do not restrict your fluid intake, but instead ensure that you drink at least 2 to 3 litres (4 to 5 pints) of water a day.

○ Cut out caffeine-containing drinks in favour of herbal teas and fruit juices.

○ Keep your salt intake down; use fresh herbs and spices to enhance the flavour of your meals. This also helps to keep your body's potassium intake high.

Rather than worrying about them, take the inevitable, outward signs of ageing (hair loss and wrinkles, for instance) as a reminder to look after yourself. As your body enters a new phase of life, eat well, keep both mentally and physically active and remain positive and full of vitality.

The menopause

The menopause is the period in a woman's life (usually between her early forties and mid-fifties) when her reproductive capacity ends, her body's oestrogen and progesterone levels drop and her body enters a new phase. Diet plays a role in the start of the menopause: the better nourished you are the later it will begin, while its symptoms (like hot flushes, dry skin, hair loss, mood swings, depression, tiredness, poor concentration, headaches, vaginal dryness and loss of sexual desire) may also be less severe. When the menopause begins, aim to eat a well-balanced diet and keep your water intake high, your alcohol consumption moderate and your caffeine intake low. Certain foods can furthermore help to alleviate some of the problems that women frequently experience during the menopause. You could try including the following foods in your diet.

o Progesterone-boosting root vegetables like sweet potatoes (Mexican yams), carrots, parsnips, potatoes and beetroot; and pulses, including chickpeas and kidney beans.

o Herbs like sarsaparilla, as well as dong quai, schizandra and white peony.

o Vitamin E-rich foods, like avocados, blackberries, mangoes, seeds and nuts.

o Fruits containing vitamin C.

o Evening-primrose and star-flower oil, which can reduce hot flushes.

After a while the body becomes used to such dietary hormonal boosts, which means that you could start experiencing problems again. If this happens, take a break from your dietary remedy for a few weeks.

Nutrition for older people

In general terms, an older person needs just as much protein, carbohydrates, vegetables, fruit, dairy products and water as a middle-aged person. Although you may be less active, the fact that your body is working less efficiently means that it needs more of a nutritional helping hand.

Keeping a food diary for a couple of weeks is a good way in which to monitor your nutrient balance. Another way in which to judge whether your body is ingesting the right amount of food is by watching your weight. If you are maintaining a steady weight, you have got the balance right. If you are gaining weight, this may either be caused by a medication that you are taking or because you are relying too heavily on high-fat foods. If you are losing weight, you are clearly not eating enough for your body's needs.

As well as keeping up your nutrient intake through a well-balanced diet, there are a few specific nutrients which you should ensure that you take, particularly vitamin D, which maintains strong bones in conjunction with calcium, and zinc.

Common health problems
Dehydration, which commonly affects older people, can cause serious health problems, such as kidney failure. If you are

worried about incontinence, stop drinking a few hours before you go to bed, and have water and other caffeine-free drinks throughout the day. If constipation is the problem, correct it by increasing your fibre and water intakes.

All too often people don't realise that the reason why they either crave foods or cannot manage to eat much is due to a side effect of medication. Keeping a food-and-symptom diary and noting the times when you take your medication should give you plenty of information on which to act. You could also ask your doctor to explain the nutritional implications of any drugs that you are taking and then boost your intake of the relevant nutrients if necessary.

Nourishing people with dementia

The best way in which to go about cooking for and feeding someone with dementia is to make a special effort to plan ahead. If you are caring for someone who has dementia, the following tips may be useful.

o Stimulate their appetite by giving them small meals and snacks; stimulate their senses by presenting food attractively; serve one-dish meals; include sensory variety within meals; and combine favourites with more nutritious foods.

o If swallowing is difficult, serve foods that are soft and easy to swallow, like omelettes and mousses, and encourage them to take small sips of a drink as they eat.

o Give them every opportunity to eat, for example, by leaving bowls of nibbles around the house, or give them nutritious drinks, like puréed-fruit milk shakes.

3. Food as a healer

What some call health, if purchased by perpetual anxiety about diet, isn't much better than tedious disease.
GEORGE DENNISON PRENTICE (1860)

Digestive problems

If you have a digestive disorder, keep a food-and-symptom diary for a couple of weeks to help you to discover whether a particular food triggers the problem.

There are a number of nutritional strategies that can help your body to get over a bout of vomiting and/or diarrhoea, as follows:

○ avoid overindulging in rich or spicy foods and alcohol;

○ drink plenty of water and non-caffeine-containing drinks;

○ substitute high-fibre foods for lower-fibre and lower-fat ones;

○ avoid raw fruits (apart from bananas) and vegetables.

Lack of fibre is the most common cause of constipation in adults, so try to eat a fibre-provider five times a day. The second most common cause is lack of water, so drink at least 2 to 3 litres (4 to 5 pints) of water every day. Cut down on your caffeine intake, too.

The presence of 'bad' bacteria in the gut is the most usual cause of wind. Taking acidophilus tablets with a couple of spoonfuls of yoghurt, or having a pot of 'live' yoghurt, containing bifidus and acidophilus, every day, can help to redress the bacterial balance. Avoid tea and coffee and instead drink mint or camomile tea or a tot of alcohol.

Eating disorders

Eating disorders are often the result of insecurities which are manifested in the need for control, often directed towards food.

It is vital that people with a disturbed body image and attitude towards food understand how their bodies work with food. Once you have understood that food has far more vital uses than simply the negative one of making you fat, it is important to try to become a little stronger.

Make a food list by dividing foods into four groups.

o A: those that you feel safe eating.

o B: those that you like and can eat a small amount of occasionally, but consider to be rather high in calories.

o C: those that you like the taste of, or idea of, eating, but won't because you think that they are too high in calories or will upset you.

o D: those that you genuinely don't like.

Build a structure into your eating pattern by having three or five small meals at roughly the same time every day. Follow recipes that make your A foods into something a little more appetising and substantial. Although your ultimate goal should be to include foods from your C group, as well as your B foods, in your diet, start by making your cooking more appetising. Take these steps gradually, and try to enjoy the experience.

Food allergies

If you think that you have a food allergy, first see your doctor in order to rule out any non-nutritional cause. After that you should look at the foods that you are eating.

Any long-term major dietary change needs professional guidance, but in the short term you can explore your diet on your own. Remove the suspected item from your diet for a week or two; if your symptoms disappear, you can probably assume that you have a sensitivity related to this food. If so, make sure that you substitute other foods for it that provide the same beneficial nutrients.

Milk, eggs, wheat and gluten and additives are most commonly responsible for food allergies.

o If you are sensitive to milk, buy products that are labelled 'milk-free' or sheep's, goats' and soya milk, yoghurt and cheese. There are some delicious varieties of cheese, such as Peccorino.

o If you have an egg sensitivity, steer clear of bought biscuits, cakes, meringues, mayonnaise, egg pasta and other manufactured foods containing albumin, lecithin and dried egg.

o In cases of wheat and gluten sensitivities, you will need to avoid wheat, barley, oats and rye, as well as products containing these, such as beer and whisky. You should also cut starch from your diet, which is found in such foods as bread, crackers, biscuits, cakes, pasta and sauces containing flour. Opt for potatoes instead.

○ If you have an additive sensitivity, you will need to examine food labels carefully. Remember that the simpler and fresher you keep your diet the fewer additives you will consume.

Fatigue

Numbered among the causes of fatigue are poor nutrition, anaemia, food intolerances, excess caffeine and alcohol. The nutritional guidelines for coping with, and curing, fatigue focus on three core issues:

○ correcting nutritional deficiencies;

○ building up a strong immune system;

○ cutting out substances from your diet that compromise your immunity and energy levels.

If you eat a well-balanced diet, and are otherwise healthy, it is very unlikely that your fatigue is caused by a vitamin or mineral deficiency. However, iron-deficiency anaemia is one of the most common causes of extreme tiredness in women. In mild cases it can be easily corrected with a diet that is rich in iron, vitamin C and other nutrients. In more severe instances your doctor or dietitian may advise you to take an iron supplement.

Some people can experience relief from fatigue by avoiding foods to which they are sensitive. Instead of following an exclusion diet, however, ensure that you have a well-balanced diet that includes plenty of fresh fruit and vegetables. Avoid snacking on sweet things and instead eat high-fibre carbohydrates, which control your sugar and energy levels better.

Caffeine overdose is a well-known cause of chronic and acute fatigue, so limit yourself to a maximum of two or three cups of good-quality tea or coffee a day. Excessive amounts of alcohol also unbalance your body nutritionally, because alcohol, like caffeine, acts as a diuretic, which causes your body to excrete vitamins and minerals.

Depression

Food alone cannot cure or prevent clinical depression, but it can do a great deal to improve your mood. Changing your eating habits can lift you out of a low period, while in more severe cases food can work in conjunction with psychotherapy and medication.

Two chemicals (neurotransmitters) within the brain specifcally affect mood: the endorphins serotonin and noradrenaline. Because the body makes these endorphins by breaking down the food that we eat, we can raise their levels in the brain by eating certain foods. Serotonin and noradrenaline are mainly derived from sugary and other carbohydrate-rich foods, but these are rapidly absorbed into the bloodstream, which results in the rapid production of insulin, causing a slump in both sugar and endorphin levels. You should therefore either have a meal as soon as possible after you eat the sugary food or consume a more slowly absorbed carbohydrate. Increase your intake of protein-rich foods, as they contain tryptophan, an amino acid which produces noradrendline and serotonin in steady, sustainabe quantities.

Depression is furthermore a common symptom of a lack of the vitamins B12 or C, or of such minerals as iron, potassium and zinc. Because depressed people have a tendency to be uninterested in food, lack of eating causes them to become deficient in such nutrients (as do some antidepressants).

The following strategies may help you to ameliorate your depression through food:

o evaluate the content of your meals and make sure that they are nutritious;

o choose foods that you can prepare easily and that you like;

o avoid drinking excessive amounts of alcohol and caffeine-containing drinks.

Headaches and migraines

By looking at the food that you eat and the way in which you live your life you can either assist your body to eradicate headaches and migraines completely, or at least become far less reliant on medication.

Although the causes of migraines are extremely complex, in simple terms they can be said to be associated with the contraction and expansion of sensitive blood vessels in the head, which creates pain. The narrowing of these blood vessels is caused by the release of the endorphin serotonin into the bloodstream, which can be triggered by a low blood-sugar level. This can be prevented by eating little and often, especially things that are both high in fibre and sweet, like fruit or a wholegrain biscuit.

Certain foods and drinks may also trigger migraines, so keep a food diary to try to discover if a certain food acts as a trigger. Many people's trigger foods are caffeine-containing drinks, red wine, cheese, chocolate or citrus fruits, particularly oranges. Others include foods containing vasoactive amines, such as processed meats and mangetout, as well as nitrates, tyramines, the flavour enhancer monosodium glutamate (MSG) and other additives, like aspartame (an artificial sweetener contained in some low-calorie drinks). Foods that are high in lactose and copper may also trigger migraines. Not all of these foods will affect you, however, and remember that fibre and water will usually cushion the effect of a trigger food.

Cholesterol and blood pressure

Nutrition plays an important part in the prevention and man-agement of both high blood cholesterol (hyperlipidaemia) and high blood pressure (hypertension).

High blood cholesterol

If you have high blood-fat levels you can decrease them by 25 per cent by adopting a healthy diet. The major principles in building a well-balanced blood scenario are as follows:

o keep your intake of saturated fats low;

o eat oily fish and garlic and drink moderate amounts of alcohol;

o follow a well-balanced diet that is rich in high-fibre foods, especially oats, and eat small meals often;

o eat plenty of foods containing beta-carotene, vitamin C and E;

o limit your intake of caffeine and nicotine.

High blood pressure

Many of the points made above about how to regulate the level of fat in your blood also apply to controlling hypertension. The following tips are important, too:

o make sure that your diet is well balanced and rich in fresh fruit and vegetables;

o eat plenty of high-fibre, starchy foods and water, smaller (but regular) amounts of lean protein and dairy products, as well as garlic, oily fish and antioxidant-containing foods;

o include only minimal quantities of salt, fat, sugar and caffeine in your diet.

Anaemia

Anaemia is an abnormal reduction of the concentration in the blood of a protein called haemoglobin, which enables the red blood cells to carry oxygen around the body.

The most common form of the condition is iron-deficiency anaemia, which may be caused by not eating enough red meat, one of the richest sources of iron. This type of anaemia is relatively easy to correct by changing the foods that you eat and your general lifestyle. For the majority of people, iron-deficiency anaemia is furthermore brought about by negative iron and vitamin C balances.

If you are anaemic, try the following strategies.

o Boost your iron intake by eating a rich source of iron two or three times a week, like a chop or steak, spaghetti bolognaise, beef Stroganoff, grilled calves' liver, lamb, venison and other game meats, like grouse and pheasant. You should also have plenty of non-haem sources of iron on most days, for example, a substantial portion of green, leafy vegetables, eggs, a lentil-, bean- or nut-based main course or dried fruits.

o Boost your vitamin C intake by eating plenty of oranges, grapefruits, cranberries and other berries, potatoes and dark-green, leafy vegetables.

o Avoid coffee, tea and cola-based drinks, as well as foods containing cereal fibre, and don't overindulge in chocolate, but remember that champagne and some red wines are rich in iron, while stout isn't.

Diabetes

There are two main types of diabetes: diabetes mellitus and diabetes insipidus, of which diabetes mellitus is the more common. The condition is characterised by an increased amount of sugar in the blood, which occurs because the pancreas does not produce enough insulin to help the body's cells to absorb the sugar.

If you are a diabetic, you should aim to achieve two major targets in your diet: to achieve and maintain control of your blood-sugar level and to keep your body weight within the ideal range. The only differences between your diet and that of a non-diabetic person is, firstly, that you need to be extra diligent about balancing it with your medication (if you take it) and, secondly, that you must be more regular in your eating habits.

The key points of a healthy diabetic dietary plan are as follows.

○ Eat plenty of high-fibre carbohydrates, which maintain a steady release of sugar into your blood.

○ Eat five portions of fresh vegetables or fruit every day; although they contain some natural sugar, their fibre content helps to regulate your blood-sugar levels.

○ Keep your intake of saturated fats to a minimum, in order to avoid developing heart disease.

○ Include dairy products in your diet, unless they are sugary products like ice cream or sweetened yoghurts.

○ Drink plenty of water, and alcohol only in moderation, and with meals, but avoid sweet wines and low-sugar beers.

○ Discuss the issue of eating sugary foods with your dietitian or doctor. The body usually copes better when they are eaten in moderation. Ideally, you should complement the sugar with fibre. If you take insulin, you should carry a sugary food with you in case your blood-sugar level drops too low.

Arthritis and gout

Correct nutrition and a well-balanced diet can bring tremendous relief to many arthritis sufferers, but different types of arthritis require different nutritional managements.

The following suggestions apply to most arthritis sufferers.

o Keep your caffeine and tannin intakes low and drink lots of water, herbal and fruit teas instead.

o Stock up your kitchen cupboards, fridge and freezer when you are feeling well so that you have plenty of healthy food to fall back on when you are going through a bad patch.

o Take any anti-inflammatory medication and painkillers with, or after, food, in order to help to minimise gastro-intestinal discomfort.

o If you suspect that your arthritis is caused by additives and preservatives, avoid ready-made, convenience and fast foods for a few weeks.

If you have rheumatoid arthritis or osteoarthritis, you may furthermore find that a diet that is rich in oily fish, or else evening-primrose oil, significantly reduces inflammation and pain.

Drug therapy using Allopurinol has largely replaced the need for dietary restriction in the treatment of gout, but you could also try limiting your intake of purines. It is not necessary to avoid all types of red meat, meat products, some types of fish, salty foods, dried fruits and beans, peas and asparagus – all of which are high in purines – but don't have too many purine sources in one day. Similarly, don't drink too much red wine, but instead boost your water intake.

Gallstones

Managing gallbladder disease is all about discovering which foods upset your body and which you can tolerate. Unless you have a genetic predisposition to developing gallstones, the best way in which to prevent and treat the disease is to make sure that you eat plenty of high-fibre foods, as these help your body to rid itself of unwanted fat and also have a cushioning effect. (Fat can cause pain and nausea because the presence of fat in the stomach stimulates the gallbladder to contract and release bile; if there are stones in the gallbladder, or its ducts are inflamed, this contraction can bring about pain.)

Try keeping a food diary for a few weeks, and if it shows that fatty foods upset your stomach, avoid them. Instead, stagger your intake of fat throughout the day and combine it with high-fibre foods. Remember that having small meals is often the best eating style, because this not only limits the pressure on the gallbladder, but also enables your body to digest food efficiently. Make sure, too, that you drink plenty of water, in order to help the fibre to work efficiently within your body.

If you have had your gallbladder removed, you will also need to address the fat content of your diet; most people find that keeping their intake of fat at a healthy level helps their digestive system to cope with it.

Cancer

Food always has a role to play in combating cancer, either as a preventative measure or as a therapy which boosts the immune system and provides the body with the nutrients that it needs, not only to fight the cancer cells but also to support cancer treatments.

There is no proof that any macrobiotic diet or other radical diet does any real good. It is better to eat a varied diet, including a regular amount of vegetables, meat, poultry, fish, cheese and eggs. Note the following advice, too.

o Eat plenty of pulses, fibre and a variety of different proteins and foods that contain antioxidant vitamins and minerals (particularly beta-carotene, vitamin C, vitamin E and selenium). Vegetables are especially rich in fibre, vitamins and minerals, and many also contain beneficial nitrates (green vegetables), folic acid, phenethyl isothiocyanate (watercress), lycopene (tomatoes) and alliums (garlic and other members of the onion family).

o Avoid eating too many chargrilled and barbecued foods, as well as an excess of fatty and sweet foods, salt and caffeine.

If you have been diagnosed with cancer, remember that there are many delicious combinations of food that will boost both your nutritional status and immune system and will make you feel empowered. Don't worry if you lose your appetite – just eat what you can, and remember that the sooner you can eat regularly again the stronger chance you will have of beating cancer.

4. The power of choice

Cook things so you can tell what they are. Good plain food ain't committed no crime an' don't need no disguise.
MARY LASSWELL (1905–94)

The discerning shopper

Many people think that the only way in which to shop healthily is to read every food packet, analysing the nutritional information given on the label. Unless you have a food-related health problem you don't need to go to this extreme, but should instead stick to buying the basic foods that you need in your diet and enjoy shopping for simple, fresh ingredients. Simple food is the secret to health and happiness!

Try to shop more often and buy less, because this will give you the opportunity to take advantage of special offers and promotions of foods in season. Avoid shopping when you're hungry, as this will cause you to dash around and make inappropriate choices. If you have the time, try to support individual shops, which can help you to choose different varieties and also offer more local produce.

Start looking at your recipe books – you'll find ideas in them that will make you think about trying out different ingredients. By enjoying experimenting in the kitchen, and looking forward to tasting new flavours in your meals, you will develop a healthy relationship with food. Think about the type of food that you really love and explore ways in which you could make it a little more exciting, as well as healthier.

Identifying real food

You'll be doing your body a huge favour by choosing and eating fresh and unadulterated food rather than heavily processed and fast food. Not only are the nutrients in real food 'packaged' in the way that nature intended, but your body will not have to deal with additives that it was not designed to digest.

Fruits, vegetables and herbs

Not only do fruits and vegetables taste better when they are in season, but the majority of vitamins and minerals disappear with time, so the sooner you eat fruits and vegetables after they have been harvested the higher their nutritional value.

There is one guideline that will help you to identify truly fresh fruits and vegetables. The seasons in the northern hemisphere are the mirror image of those in the southern hemisphere, which means that while British apples traditionally crop in autumn (September to October), South African apples crop in May to July. If you are buying apples in July, you should therefore choose a southern-hemisphere apple (from South Africa or New Zealand) rather than a northern-hemisphere, British or French one.

Although supermarkets sell herbs growing in pots (which stay fresh for longer than packs of cut herbs), it is better to grow your own, as you can pick only what you need and they couldn't be any fresher.

Meat, game and poultry

Following the health scares of recent years, your best bet is to choose organic beef approved by Soil Association farmers who maintain organic standards, use natural food with which to feed their cattle and no growth-promoting drugs, and who are ultimately concerned with animal welfare. The best beef comes from animals that are about eighteen months old, but this must be matured, or 'hung', for ten to twenty days at low temperatures in order to tenderise it and improve its flavour and keeping qualities. The lean meat on properly hung beef should be a deep-plum-red colour and slightly moist. It should have a good outer covering of fat, creamy to pale yellow in colour and of firm texture.

The tastiest and healthiest pork comes from pigs that have been kept outside and allowed the freedom to live as natural a life as possible. The best pork should be pink, smooth and firm to the touch; freshly cut surfaces should look slightly moist and there should be no excessive fat. The fat should be firm and a clear, milky white in colour; avoid cuts with soft, grey and oily fat. The skin, or rind, should be thin, pliable, smooth and free of hairs.

Choosing good lamb is relatively simple. Lambs cannot be factory farmed and their pasture is not normally sprayed, so most lamb is free from chemical residues. The time of year when slaughtering takes place affects the appearance of the meat: good-quality, winter lamb is dark red, with creamy, marbled fat, while spring lamb is slightly lighter (dark pink), with white fat.

Although many types of game are commercially frozen and therefore available all year round, the flavour is at its best in freshly killed and well-hung game, which is available in autumn and winter. It is best to purchase game from a reputable butcher who knows the origins and hanging times of the meat that he is selling.

The best-tasting and most nutritious poultry comes from birds that have been given space in which to exercise and make nests, with natural light and natural feed (like grain), and that are slaughtered when they are mature, which improves their taste. Unless poultry is labelled 'free range' you should assume that the bird has been reared in less than ideal conditions, and I would not advise you to buy it.

Eggs

We cannot expect hens that are being kept under the appallingly stressful conditions of battery farms to produce decent eggs, but whether you are concerned with animal welfare or the taste of real food you should always buy free-range eggs, organic if possible.

Fish and shellfish

The drawback to buying fresh fish is that it should be bought on the day that it is to be eaten, which is not always viable. When buying fresh fish, look for bright, rounded eyes (dull and sunken eyes are a bad sign), red (not greyish) gills, firm flesh and a sea-fresh smell (it is the 'fishy' smell of fish that is past its best that puts many people off it). Although frozen fish is usually inferior in terms of taste, it can be quite acceptable in casseroles and soups. Canned fish can be kept in the store cupboard for simple supper dishes.

Remember that because harvests fluctuate so should availability. If the same shellfish is always sold it is likely to be frozen (some varieties lose their succulent tenderness and delicate flavour and become rubbery and bland when frozen). Never eat molluscs that you've harvested yourself, because water conditions are very unreliable and they are likely to be riddled with toxins.

Dairy products

Antibiotics and pollutants can easily be passed into milk, so if you want to avoid them drink organic milk. Organic butter similarly offers the best taste and limits your potential exposure to chemical residues. In the case of yoghurt, again opt for organic products and choose plain – rather than fruit-flavoured – yoghurts, which are additive-free (you can always add your own chopped, puréed or stewed fruit).

When buying cheese, make sure that it is appropriately wrapped and not wrinkling or drying at the edges. Hard cheeses should look smooth, with no large, dry cracks, while soft cheeses should look moist, not withered. The cheese should smell inviting rather than either odourless or, if strong smelling, rancid or reeking of ammonia. Farmhouse and hand-made cheeses are usually worth buying, as are those whose labels use the French abbreviation AOC (*Appellation d'Origine Contrôlée*), which means that their provenance has been strictly controlled.

Interpreting food labels

Here are some points to remember when examining food labels.

○ When you buy food whose label gives no information about how it was grown, or that is not labelled 'organic', you should assume that it was produced with the aid of chemicals.

○ The sugar content of food can be disguised with the names fructose, maltose, lactose, dextrose, sucrose, glucose, honey, concentrated fruit juice and 'syrup'. 'Sugar-free' may simply mean that a food does not contain sucrose, while 'no added sugar' means that it is naturally sweet.

○ Foods labelled 'low fat', 'low sugar' and 'diabetic' may contain huge amounts of salt, while salt (sodium chloride) is often listed as sodium on labels.

○ 'Slimline' foods can contain as much as 40 per cent fat; low-fat foods may contain enormous amounts of sugar; and low-sugar foods may contain more fat than the standard version of the food.

Additives often appear after the food ingredients on food labels, grouped under their category headings and itemised by their code number, full chemical name, or both. Here is a brief guide to what the jargon on the label really means.

○ Antioxidants (E300 to E321): additives that delay or prevent food from turning rancid or changing in taste, smell and appearance.

○ Colourings (E100 to E180): additives that impart a

characteristic or appetising colour to foods or intensify the colour. About half the permitted colours are extracts from natural sources, the rest are man-made.

○ Emulsifiers, stabilisers and thickeners (E322 to E495): additives that affect the texture of foods.

○ Enriched: some of the nutrients lost during processing have been put back into the food.

○ Flavour enhancers (E620 to E632): additives that modify the taste or smell of food without imparting a flavour of their own. The most important of these are monosodium glutamate, or MSG (E621), and its relatives, E620 to E623.

○ Flavourings: there are over 2,000 of these; many are herbs and spices, but a lot are man-made. Unlike other additives, they do not have to be itemised on food labels and do not have E numbers.

○ Preservatives (E200 to E283): additives that help to prevent the deterioration of the food product until its 'sell by' or 'best before' date.

○ RDA: the recommended daily amount, or allowance, as specified by the British government, that an adult should consume in order to avoid developing any type of nutritional deficiency.

○ Sweeteners: artificial sweeteners that have a sweet taste, but few, if any, calories.

Keeping a food diary

By keeping a food diary you can often attribute worrying symptoms to an excess of a certain food or drink or a lack of an essential nutrient. A food diary can also inspire you to look afresh at your eating habits.

Record everything that you eat and drink for at least seven days. Write down what you have consumed and how it was prepared as soon as possible after eating it. If you eat foods from packets or tins, and you suspect that they may contain an additive that upsets you, you will need to record details of all of their ingredients and additives.

You should also record the quantity of everything that you eat and drink. Don't worry about exact measurements in ounces or grams, but write down whether you ate a breast or slice of chicken, for example. This will not only give you an idea of whether you are eating too little or too much, but will also enable you to juggle the quantities of food that you eat if you are worried about a food intolerance or allergy.

Finally, you should record how you are feeling. It is also worth noting exactly why you are eating or drinking – for instance, are you hungry, stressed or eating for comfort? The answers to these questions will tell you a lot about the emotional aspects of your eating habits.